Cat Urine Odor Solutions

Morgen Marshall

Marshall Press
Johnson City, TN, USA

ISBN-13:
978-09848883-3-7

ISBN-10:
0984888330

DEDICATION

In memory of Beasley

CONTENTS

ACKNOWLEDGMENTS

Liz Schmidt helped me with the original concept and art.
Gary at Bio Fog helped me with their product SCOE-10X
Many customers and readers at For the Love of Cats were
helpful in developing my voice and concepts. I especially
thank Ken Evoy of Sitesell, Inc. for helping me to find my
passion.

THE NUMBER ONE OFFENDER

Cat Urine Odor is the Number One Offender for Cat Owners!
More cats lose their homes or are euthanized because of Urine Odor
than for any other reason.

Thankfully, though, there are a number of ways to tackle cat urine odor problems – they're simple solutions and easy to implement, making certain that you and your furperson can live together lovingly!

Cats are naturally fastidious and clean, so if they go outside the litter box, there is a reason. The first place to start is to confine the cat and deodorize. Once this is done, you set about to discover the reason for the problem – if you take away the reason, you're much closer to solving the problem.

A Note:

I recommend using clumping litter if you can. It throws less dust and it is easier to keep the litter box clean. As a bonus, you only need to add litter to the litter box as it clumps, and is removed. When the litter stops clumping properly, or the urine clumps stick to the box a little too well and break apart upon removal, then dump the box, completely clean it with warm soap and water, and put in fresh litter.

Some folks have a problem with clumping litter, and so do some cats. If that is the case, use your best judgment – but you will need to scoop all hard soil from the box daily during re-training.

Change the box at least once a week, too. Don't allow the urine to build up and turn to ammonia. If the weather is warmer than usual or it is the warm time of year, change the box twice a week.

Nothing is more offensive to you and your cat – and kitty is much closer to the source of the odor and has a more sensitive nose than humans, than urine that has turned to ammonia in the litter box. Don't insult your cat in this way.

Some Examples to Consider:
Begin by having your beloved kitty checked by the vet for urinary tract problems. If there is no infection or defect, then you know the problem is behavioral and can be addressed by the methods I outline.

Look around your home. Has there been a change in the household in the last few months? A new person or pet? Has someone left the home or passed away? Is there a new partnership? What has happened in your home lately? How long has the behavior been going on? Next, what is your cat soiling? Is it the rug, the laundry, or your bed? Let's look at each scenario separately:

Example #1:	A new cat moved in with you and your cat is going on the floor outside the box, but near it.
Example #2:	An animal is visiting outdoors and your cat is "marking" near doors, windows and other parts of the carpet and walls.
Example #3:	Your child has left for college or a member of the family has passed. Your cat is despondent and going all over the house.
Example #4:	You have a new mate and your cat is going in the closet or on your bed.
Example #5:	You have a new puppy and your cat is going all over the house instead of the litter box.
Example #6:	You had an addition to the family – foster children, baby or visiting family members. Your cat is dragging feces all over the house or just going where ever she happens to be.
Example #7:	You left for a weekend and the litter box got dirty and now your cat won't use it.
Example #8:	You got a new, expensive, self-cleaning litter box and your cat used it once and now won't use it at all.
Example #9:	You recently got the cat and it won't use a litter box and you want to give it back.
Example #10:	You moved to a new house and now your cat is always going on the floor in the same place and refuses to stop.
Example #11:	Your cat was recently declawed and will no longer use the litter box.
Example #12:	Your cat who used to use the litter box happily and correctly is now always "missing" the box, but you always see it go to the box.
Example #13:	Your cat had a urinary tract infection or other medical condition and equates the litter box with the pain of the condition.
Example # 14	Your cat went to a kennel and now it no longer will use the litter box.

I'm sure there are other examples, as well. Don't give up, no matter what!

RE-TRAINING AND DEODORIZING

The solution is nearly always the same to start – confine the cat and deodorize the area.   The actual mechanics of re-training your cat to the litter box aren't that difficult. They are almost intuitive – but identifying the behaviors or environmental factors that drove your cat to going outside the box is not always so easy.

So, figure out the problem that caused the behavior and adjust the environment to eliminate the cause.   When the cat is using the litter box without mishap, allow it out of confinement and watch for a few days.   If there are no accidents, then all is well.   If things start up again, you know something is still wrong.

So, this little book is to help you to figure out what is wrong for your cat and to fix things for this trying set of symptoms.   Most common causes are addressed, but there are other causes that happen so rarely, they won't be listed here.   That's where I come in.   I work with cat owners around the world, fixing the broken behaviors that make cats so difficult to live with at times.

Let's go through this two-step process of re-training and deodorizing, and then we will go back to the examples above and address each one separately.

Retraining

Step 1)   Put the cat in a small room with a hard floor – usually the bathroom or utility room – with a clean litter box, food and water bowls, bedding if your cat is not soiling it already, and some toys. Your cat will remain in this room for at least three (3) days. Other pets may visit your cat, but your cat may not come out and the visiting pets must be immediately removed if they try to approach the litter box.

Go into this room and visit your cat and snuggle and play with it as often as you want to or can. You, as the primary caretaker of the cat, will also have to clean the litter box morning and night without fail.

When you go in to clean the box, you need to exaggerate your movements and make a big deal about cleaning the box. This exaggerated behavior will draw attention to your actions and show kitty that you want a clean litter box just as much as she does. Don't grumble! If you grumble, kitty knows it. Just cheerfully clean the box with as much "hammy, bad acting" as you can muster.

Praise your cat for any soil you find in the box and remove. The more you praise your cat, the faster your cat will "get it" that using the box is the right thing to do.

If there are any misses, distract your cat with a toy or some food and quietly clean up the mess. Do not scold or otherwise say anything to your cat.

Deodorizing

Step 2)   Deodorize the house. Urine is very alkaline – like sulfuric acid or lye. It crystallizes as it dries and can grind and cut fibers, such as carpet or bedding. Washing with general detergents is not enough. Urine is an organic stain, and holds on very hard to all fabrics and natural surfaces.

Deodorizing is not that mystical, but many folks are just lost here. You have basically one (1) product and one tool that are absolutely necessary. There are optional products, depending on your situation. There are many products on the market, but a lot of them are a lot better at taking your money than deodorizing. I only recommend products and processes that actually work.

Necessary Products for Deodorizing:

Microbe Clean – an enzymatic cleaner
Or,
White Vinegar (distilled 5% acid, cooking vinegar is fine)
Or,
SCOE 10-X – a probiotic deodorizing treatment, made by BioFog in GA, USA
And,
Handheld UV Light – to help you find the spots that need treatment

Optional Deodorizing Products:
KOE – for use in kennels
Laundry Detergent and deodorizers such as Borateem or Laundry Saver or White Vinegar
Skunk Remover – for outdoor use
For-Bid for Dogs – to stop your dog from eating feces from the litter box

Sources for each of the products are at the end of this book. I would rather tell you how to use them first, so that you can get only the items you need and not waste your time or money. Read through the directions in this section and then compare the Example scenarios to your situation.

Once you decide which is likely to work best for you, you can then purchase the products. However, don't wait around too long – your cat is only going to be in isolation for three (3) days, and you still need to have many of the items shipped to you!

If your home is not deodorized prior to your cat being released from confinement, you are likely going to see your cat go back to the same areas and continue the behaviors – purely because of smell.

To deodorize your home, start by wiping up any wet mess or urine. Once you have most of it up, take a quart of clean water and add ¼ cup of white vinegar to it. (2 liters and ¼ liter). Take the solution and wet down the area that had urine on it – go twice the size of the original wet spot. Allow to dry.

For carpeted areas, get out your carpet cleaner and go over the carpet using the extractor only, then use the vinegar solution as the washing solution. Once you extract the wet vinegar solution, allow it to dry. Use your UV light and check the floor and walls as high as your knees. Any spots that glow bright are organic matter – likely urine. These are the spots you will concentrate on for the next steps.

Take either the Microbe Clean or the SCOE 10x and go over the spots – and increase the size of the treatment to at least twice the size of the spots – and allow it to dry without heat or other help. However, a fan may be used. Be sure to follow the instructions on the bottle. The products act differently, so follow the directions carefully. Results can only be guaranteed if you do. If one treatment doesn't work for you, read the directions for removing any residue and start over using something else.

Once the spots are dry, use your UV light again. You should not see any spots that glow brightly, but there may be some areas that seem brighter than others. If you see a large smeary area on hard flooring, the area needs to be stripped of any floor treatments and deodorized again. When the treatment dries, seal the floor again.

Sometimes, the only thing to do is replace the subflooring in a house. To do this, you must remove all floor coverings, such as rugs or laminate flooring and remove sheets of plywood to expose the joists beneath. Treat the joists with one of the products above and seal the wood with a good primer.

Then, rebuild the flooring to match the rest of the house. This only needs to be done in extreme cases where the urine has soaked through flooring repeatedly and not been addressed. It may happen in rental properties or abandoned properties or you may have purchased the problem with the property.

SOME EXAMPLES

Some Examples of Behavioral Causes and Conditions

Example #1:
A new cat moved in with you and your cat is going on the floor outside the box, but near it.

Your cat may not like to share the box. Male cats each need their own litter box. Females will naturally share, but males need their own box. If you have two females, it is likely that the new cat is surprising your original cat in the litter box and she does not feel secure. I normally do not recommend covered litter boxes, but in this case, it may be helpful. You can use a large storage box and cut a slot in the side from just below the rim to 4" above the bottom – straight sides are fine. And fill the storage box with litter to within 1"from the opening you just cut. Put the lid on and voila'! You have a covered litter box that is large enough for the largest Maine Coon cat.

Example #2:
An animal is visiting outdoors and your cat is "marking" near doors, windows and other parts of the carpet and walls.

The visitor cat is likely spraying and marking outside, causing your indoor cat to feel threatened, hence the counter-marking. Deodorize the house indoors around all openings and the joint of floor to walls, continuing up the walls as high as your knees. Once the deodorizing is done on the inside, you need to do the outside. Use the Skunk Remover and spray a 10-foot swath from knee-high on the outside of the building in a continuous perimeter.

Example #3:
Your child has left for college or a member of the family has passed. Your cat is despondent and going all over the house.

Your cat is depressed and despondent. I suggest reading about cat grief. Talk to your cat and comfort it. Your cat needs love and care. Share your grief and loss with your cat. Retraining can be done, and the deodorizing should be done. Be sure to play with and love your cat through this depression.

To address the grief, try visualizing the person or pet that is no longer around as you hold your cat and comfort it. I believe that cats can see a clearly visualized image in our minds because I've seen this help so many times. I use this little tool in all phases of training with cats.

Example #4:
You have a new mate and your cat is going in the closet or on your bed.

This is one of the most objectionable of all behaviors.

First off, wash all washable items with Laundry Detergent using all the deodorizers listed in the products section. Use white vinegar in a separate rinse cycle to be sure to remove all the odors. If your cat is going on the bed, you will need to strip the bed and treat the mattress with spray-on products.

The behaviors are likely caused by your mate. If your sex life is particularly noisy, your cat may feel that you are in danger. If you pay more attention to your mate instead of your cat, like your cat is used to, your cat may be jealous. Each situation is slightly different.

Now, there is a delicate situation – if your mate does not appreciate your cat! The cat may use any and all tactics to get your attention. Remember that your cat loves you and is used to you being all hers – and now you have a mate and kitty is relegated to second fiddle. No one likes to be thrown over – not even a cat. Especially when a new person in the home does not appreciate the feline kind.

Train your new mate to appreciate your cat while you re-train your cat to the litter box. Both will be happier in the long run. Besides, your cat knows if your mate is a good person or not, even better than you do! Trust her intuition!

If your new mate just will not tolerate your cat, replace your mate. Seriously! Who wants to go through life without cats?

Example #5:
You have a new puppy and your cat is going all over the house instead of the litter box.

This situation is rather involved – get your cat a tree that is tall enough to look down on all and sundry. Your cat needs a clear path to the litter box and a way to get away from the dog. Make sure that you keep the puppy out of the litter box. Many dogs like to eat feces (there is a product made just for this condition!) and when you get a pup, it is likely not trained yet to leave kitties alone. If kitty has a place to look down on things, it can train the dog correctly.

Now, the litter box needs to be protected until your new dog is well trained. I suggest using any means necessary to give your cat a clear path to the litter box at all times.

Example #6:
You had an addition to the family – foster children, baby or visiting family members. Your cat is dragging feces all over the house or just going where ever she happens to be.

This poor kitty is stressed to the max. It is likely that your cat cannot sleep or find a quiet spot. The children need to be advised – or told or ordered or whatever – to leave kitty alone. Stereos need to be kept quiet. See the new puppy example in #5. You can also give your cat a covered hidey-hole bed to help her feel more secure.

Example #7:
You left for a weekend and the litter box got dirty and now your cat won't use it.

It's likely that the plastic is stained and ruined. I suggest getting a new litter box and see how things go. You can "season" the box by putting a little urine smell on the inside of the rim. You can also smear a little feces on the inside of the rim to draw your kitty to the box.

If your cat does not use the litter box after three days of confinement, change the litter type. If you are using perfumed litter, try a litter with no perfume. If you are using clay, try clumping. If you are using clumping, try crystals, or wheat hulls, or something else. Change your litter type. Completely clean the litter box, and put the new litter in. Give each change in litter 3 days to see how your cat likes it.

Some cats are adversely affected by clumping litters. I've even heard some veterinarians say that cats prone to hairballs that the hairballs can be much worse using clumping litter. If this seems the case for your cats, change the litter type and see how they do.

Example #8:
You got a new, expensive, self-cleaning litter box and your cat used it once and now won't use it at all.

It is likely that your cat got scared off the box. I suggest adjusting the timer to the longest setting available. Start by setting up the box without the self-cleaning option. Allow your cat to use this for at least 3 days prior to connecting the self-cleaner. Once your cat is using the box correctly again, you can allow your cat out of confinement.

Example #9:
You recently got the cat and it won't use a litter box and you want to give it back.

It is likely that your cat had this problem when it arrived at the shelter. You inherited this problem with the cat. More than likely, this is the cause of your cat being in the shelter to begin with. Your job is to train the cat to the litter box. Don't worry about how long it takes, just keep at it. Your cat had a scare or was terrorized early on, and is likely very resistant to using a litter box.

As an alternative, you might put your cat outdoors. If your

cat is de-clawed, don't do this, but keep trying instead. The rewards can be much greater for both of you. If you give the cat back to where you got it, the chances are good it won't be given another chance at a home, ever. Try to find a solution before you give up. If you are reading this book, I'm sure you are the kind of person who will do anything to help feline kind, so please give the poor kitty a chance. Read #14, too.

Example #10:
You moved to a new house and now your cat is always going on the floor in the same place and refuses to stop.

If your cat is using the same spots no matter what you do, it is likely that the sub-flooring is affected. You will need to strip the flooring (carpet or tile or whatever – usually carpet and padding) and then either replace or treat the sub-flooring. I suggest you cut the section of sub-flooring out and replace it. The carpet and padding you removed will need to be replaced, as well.

If this project seems daunting to you, call a contractor. Likely the prior tenants or an ill-mannered dog used that spot repeatedly and destroyed the sub-flooring.

Example #11:
Your cat was recently declawed and will no longer use the litter box.

The reason this cat won't use the litter box is pain. Go to the hardware store and get some play sand. It's usually sterile, or close to it. The grains are fine enough that they likely will not hurt your cat's feet. Do not remove the bandages. Allow the feet to completely heal in the bandages before you remove them. It will take several months for the feet to be calloused enough to use regular litter. Be sure to keep the litter box clean so that your cat does not develop any infections during the healing period.

Example #12:
Your cat, who used to use the litter box happily and correctly is now always "missing" the box, but you always see it go to the box.

Your cat has likely outgrown the litter box – the box is too small or the cat likes to stand to urinate. I suggest changing from a regular litter box to a large storage bin – at least 35 gallon size, and tossing the lid. Try to find one with a flat bottom for ease of cleaning – and get the largest you can find. Something with high sides, the wrapping paper or sweater box for under the bed is not going to help.

Put fresh litter in the box and replace the existing litter box with your new box. Watch kitty get used to it, jumping in and out. When kitty backs up, he runs into the wall, and feels secure spraying his urine, knowing it will hit the litter at his feet. Kitty will thank you!

Example #13:
Your cat had a urinary tract infection or other medical condition and equates the litter box with the pain of the condition.

Your cat needs to be retrained to the box. Follow directions for this and also check your cat's urine at least once a month using a special litter or an additive that alerts you to the condition. You may also want to deodorize the house or just the spots your cat has been using. That is up to you – but watch your cat to be sure that after 3 days in confinement, it doesn't go back to urinating outside the litter box. You need to be especially nice to your cat when it uses the litter box during confinement – just no treats.

Example #14:
Your cat went to a kennel and now it will no longer use the litter box.

This is a heartbreaking situation because you had nothing to do with the cause and we can't know the cause for sure. Retrain the cat to the box using the most gentle methods you can and try very hard not to be discouraged. It may become apparent that your cat will never use the box again. Fill the tub and sink with a little water to discourage the cat from urinating in these facilities and keep at it.

Some cats will poop all over the floor but urinate in the box, while others will urinate all over the place but poop in the box. It's confusing. The behavior that developed at the kennel was likely to show objection of the situation and force the kennel owner, whom your cat thought was a new owner who kept cats in cages, to give her back to you. Since she did get to go back home to you, she may feel this behavior is successful, and therefore continue it. Try to be patient and know that your cat loves you very much.

If you have not seen it, take a look at the book "The Cat's House." They offer excellent ideas for paths out of harm's way that will lead directly to the litter box.

http://www.thecatshouse.com

PRODUCT INFORMATION AND SOURCES

Microbe Clean – an enzymatic cleaner
This is available at PetCo, Amazon and online. It is the only enzymatic cleaner I recommend. The by-product is water, so it is safe around children and pets.

SCOE 10-x – a probiotic deodorizing treatment
This product was developed by a janitorial company and is actually guaranteed to remove all organic odors from building materials. The link will take you to their testimonial page, so read all about it and then give it a try. It truly is amazing. You need to follow directions carefully or the guarantee is void. The product is only available from the manufacturer/developer, online. http://www.scoe10x.com

KOE – for use in kennels
Also called "Kennel Odor Eraser." This is for cement, tile, stone, and other hard surfaces. It helps breeders and kennels to keep clean, disinfected and deodorized. It cleans as well as deodorizes. The product is non-toxic around pets when allowed to dry completely. It can be found at some specialty stores, and online.

Laundry Soap, Borateem and White Vinegar
These products can be found in most grocery stores. Just remember to not wash anything with urine on it with chlorine bleach. Go through getting the urine our first. Urine turns to ammonia (that objectionable odor!) as it dries. It is not a good idea to combine these, as the mixing of ammonia and chlorine bleach creates a toxic fume that can hurt you.

Skunk Remover – for outdoor use
This is for use outdoors, when you have a visitor animal spraying and disturbing your indoor cats. It does need to be re-applied after a rain, but it lasts a long time. After use, you will still have visitor cats, but the smell of the spray (or the musk of mating) will no longer be evident.

You get to decide what to do about the visitors. It can also be used on a dog or other property when a skunk has sprayed. It is non-toxic and safe for use. This is available at specialty suppliers, janitorial supply and online. Many large pet supply providers carry it.

Portable UV Light – to help you find the spots that need treatment
This is a 6-inch long UV or "blacklight" unit that is hand-held. There are battery-operated and plug-in models available. Usually, the battery-operated units are more convenient. They are available on eBay and Amazon, among other sources. Try a large pet supply store near you first to save yourself the extra cost of shipping it to you.

For-Bid Feces Deterrent – for your dog
If your dog wants to eat feces from the litter box, this product makes them un-appetizing so you can train your dog away from them. Your cat will thank you, also. And your wife and kids will thank you, too! Who wants a dog

licking their face after it's been in the litter box? You can find it at specialty pet supply stores. I believe Tractor Supply Stores also carry it.

ABOUT THE AUTHOR

Morgen Marshall is an avid cat lover with a lifetime experience of cats of all kinds. She sheltered foster cats and helped them to their new homes for a while, and ran the website "for-the-love-of-cats" for seven years, helping cat owners all over the world to care for their cats. She also helped many would-be veterinarians enter the highly competitive veterinarian schools in the US.

She may be found on facebook in the group for the love of cats, bit.ly/1W2v017.

Ms. Marshall lives in the Tri-Cities area with two rescue cats, Princess and Queenie. She is a teacher and healer by temperament.

www.ingramcontent.com/pod-product-compliance
Lightning Source LLC
LaVergne TN
LVHW051207080426
835508LV00021B/2857